Suzanne Collins'

Mockingjay

The Hunger Games – Book Three

BookCaps™ Study Guide

www.bookcaps.com

© 2011. All Rights Reserved.

Table of Contents

HISTORICAL CONTEXT 4

PLOT..6

CHARACTERS..8
- Katniss Everdeen 8
- Peeta Mellark 9
- Gale Hawthorne..10
- Prim Everdeen 11
- Haymitch Abernathy 12
- President Coin 12
- President Snow 13
- Plutarch Heavensbee 14
- Beetee 15
- Finnick Odair 16
- Johanna Mason 17
- Boggs 17
- Cressida 18
- Pollux 18
- Annie Cresta 19

THEMES 20

CHAPTER SUMMARIES 26
- Chapter One...27
- Chapter Two 29
- Chapter Three 31
- Chapter Four 33
- Chapter Five 35
- Chapter Six 37
- Chapter Seven 39
- Chapter Eight...41
- Chapter Nine..43
- Chapter Ten 45

CHAPTER ELEVEN 47
CHAPTER TWELVE 49
CHAPTER THIRTEEN 51
CHAPTER FOURTEEN 53
CHAPTER FIFTEEN 55
CHAPTER SIXTEEN 57
CHAPTER SEVENTEEN 59
CHAPTER EIGHTEEN 61
CHAPTER NINETEEN 63
CHAPTER TWENTY 65
CHAPTER TWENTY-ONE 67
CHAPTER TWENTY-TWO 69
CHAPTER TWENTY-THREE 71
CHAPTER TWENTY-FOUR 73
CHAPTER TWENTY-FIVE 75
CHAPTER TWENTY-SIX 77
CHAPTER TWENTY-SEVEN 79
ABOUT BOOKCAPS 81

Historical Context

Suzanne Collins was born in Connecticut in 1962. In the 1990's, she wrote from some children's television shows on the Nickelodeon network. While working on a kids' show called "Generation O!" she met writer James Proimos who inspired her to begin writing children's novels. Her first novel, "Gregor the Overlander" was the first in a series of critically acclaimed books known as the Underland Chronicles and was inspired by Alice in Wonderland.

The Underland Chronicles were published between 2003 and 2007 and earned Collins notoriety in the literary world. In 2008 "The Hunger Games" was published as the first book in a trilogy that was followed up by "Catching Fire" (2009) and "Mockingjay" (2010); the trilogy has been wildly successful.

Collins' idea for the books of the Hunger Games series came from watching reality television, reading war coverage, and influencing from the times of gladiator battles. The world of Panem, where the novels take place, is a dystopian society in the future where all of the "districts" in which people are dictated by the President who lives in the Capitol; a place far different from the poor districts which exist solely to provide goods for those who live in the Capitol. Every year the Capitol takes two teenagers from each district as tributes to compete in the Hunger Games, a gladiator-type reality show where only one tribute comes back alive. Katniss Everdeen, the heroine of the series, begins a battle against the Capitol that propels itself to a catastrophic degree in an effort to live a life of freedom.

Plot

After being rescued from the Quarter Quell by a District 13 hovercraft Katniss has learned that District 12 has been destroyed and Peeta has been taken by the Capitol. Katniss is taken to District 13 where she is amazed to learn of the underground world that has existed in District 13 ever since the district was supposedly destroyed and is being led by its own president, President Coin.

District 13 Katniss finds it hard to focus on the strict schedule she is given and her task as the Mockingjay, the face of the rebellion, because she is too worried about Peeta. As the Capitol begins airing interviews with an increasingly lifeless Peeta, Katniss becomes even more worried about him, and it fuels her desire to contribute to the rebellion.

Katniss, Finnick, and Gale film television spots that Beetee manages to interrupt Capitol broadcasts with and they visit the other districts that are in various stages of rebellion so Katniss, the Mockingjay, can give them hope. After Peeta tips Katniss off about an attack on television District 13 decides to rescue him and to hide further underground. To Katniss' dismay Peeta has been brainwashed by the Capitol and not only distrusts her when arrives in 13, he tries to kill her more than once.

A group of rebels from 13 including Katniss, Gale, Peeta, Johanna, and others decides to enter the Capitol so Katniss can kill President Snow herself. They face many obstacles along the way, and most of the rebel party is killed. Once in the Capitol Katniss suffers the loss of her sister, Prim, at the hands of District 13 and rather than killing President Snow publically, as she is set to do, she turns her bow and arrow on President Coin.

After the Capitol and Coin are both taken down Katniss is free to return to her home in Victor's Village of District 12 though neither Gale nor Mrs. Everdeen join her; but Peeta does.

Characters

Katniss Everdeen

Katniss has survived the 74th Hunger Games and was rescued from the Quarter Quell. Now she is brought to the very strict District 13 where she is told that a rebellion has formed, and she is the face of the rebellion, the Mockingjay. Katniss does not want to lead the rebellion until she realizes that Peeta is being tortured in the Capitol and she makes it her mission to save him, and then to kill President Snow. Katniss works with the rebellion until she realizes that President Coin is not her ally, but her enemy. Katniss suffers great losses in this final installment and finally gains an understanding of her feelings for Peeta and Gale.

Peeta Mellark

Peeta has been taken from the Quarter Quell and taken to the Capitol where he is tortured and forced to record interviews that air all over Panem. Peeta is brainwashed into believing that Katniss is the enemy and when he is finally reunited with her he tries to kill her. Peeta joins the rebel group that is to take down the Capitol and along the way the rebels try to help him remember who he was, especially Katniss and Gale as they knew him the best out of everyone. Peeta wants to die because he feels he is a hindrance to everyone but Katniss will not allow it and eventually realizes she loves him.

Gale Hawthorne

Gale becomes a very important and active member of the rebellion while he resides in District 13 and forms a close relationship with President Coin. Katniss remains good friends with Gale though it seems obvious that things will never be the same between them ever since Peeta has come into the picture. Gale works with Beetee to formulate a set of snares for humans that they feel will be beneficial to the rebellion, but when one of those snares kills Prim Katniss can no longer trust Gale or look at him in the same way. After the rebellion is over, Gale does not return to District 12.

Prim Everdeen

Prim is the younger sister of Katniss, and, in District 13, she begins to be trained as a doctor. Prim works with Mrs. Everdeen in the hospital and is on hand to treat anyone with injuries or illness, and also to comfort Katniss when she is feeling lost without Peeta. Prim has grown up tremendously throughout the series, and Katniss develops a great deal of respect and pride for her. Prim is killed while tending to sick children in the Capitol and Katniss finds out that District 13, not the Capitol, is responsible for her death.

Haymitch Abernathy

Haymitch is an integral part of the rebellion and Katniss is at first very upset with him for not telling her about District 13 or the plan to rescue her from the Quarter Quell, and also with the fact that they did not rescue Peeta. Katniss is forced to listen to Haymitch, however, if the rebellion is to go on smoothly. It is learned that Haymitch's entire family and also his girlfriend were killed by the Capitol after his turn in the Hunger Games because he had used the force field as a weapon, which was considered a slap in the face to the Capitol.

President Coin

President Coin is the leader of District 13 and makes all decisions when it comes to the rebellion, despite Katniss' obvious distrust of her. She runs 13 with a very strict precision and perfection, which alerts Katniss to her hunger for the same power she is trying to take down in the Capitol. President Coin's willingness to lie to those who trust her and her determination to achieve the power she so desperately seeks ultimately lead to her demise at Katniss' hands.

President Snow

President Snow has been a symbol of everything that Katniss is against since the beginning of the series, but, in this final installment, she realizes that while she hates him, she can trust him. She hates everything he stands for and especially despises him for torturing Peeta, but she knows that Snow will always stick to his word, and tell her exactly what he thinks, even if she does not agree with it. Snow is the one who tells Katniss that it was a District 13 trap that killed Prim, not one set by the Capitol, and she realizes that Coin is her true enemy.

Plutarch Heavensbee

Plutarch was the head gamemaker during the Quarter Quell and orchestrated the rescue of Katniss and the other rebels. Plutarch has the idea to create propaganda videos featuring Katniss and the other rebels that will air throughout the districts and interrupt Capitol broadcasts. He is an important figure in the rebellion and one who Katniss trusts because he does not seem to have a thirst for power so much as a thirst for freedom. He does not brag about his accomplishments and when the rebellion is over he becomes the Secretary of Communications for Panem.

Beetee

Beetee was rescued from the Quarter Quell arena with Katniss and Finnick and becomes instrumental in the rebellion because of his knowledge of electronics and weaponry. He creates special bow and arrows for Katniss and Gale and even a special trident for Finnick. Beetee and Gale work together to create a series of snares that will trap humans and hopefully aid them in the rebellion, though one of those snares is used to kill rebels, like Prim.

Finnick Odair

Finnick is a good friend of Katniss in "Mockingjay" and they film propaganda spots together to encourage the rebels. It is revealed that Finnick was used as a prostitute by President Snow after he won the Hunger Games and he vows to get his revenge. When Peeta is rescued from the Capito,l so is Finnick's girlfriend, Annie Cresta and soon Finnick and Annie are married. When the group of rebels including Finnick and Katniss heads to the Capitol Finnick is unable to escape some mutant lizards and is killed. At the end of the novel, we learn that Annie was pregnant when Finnick died.

Johanna Mason

Johanna was in the Quarter Quell and Katniss thought Johanna tried to kill her, though she was just digging the tracking device out of Katniss' arm. Johanna and Katniss never really got along, but when Johanna was rescued from the Capitol and brought to District 13 she and Katniss trained together so they could join the rebel troops and became friends. Johanna reveals that President Snow had nothing to torture her with mentally because he already killed her family so he tortured her physically instead, with electric shocks.

Boggs

Boggs is introduced as one of President Coin's guards in District 13, but he quickly becomes important to the rebellion and important to Katniss. Katniss likes Boggs because he is very friendly and has a decent sense of humor. Boggs serves as a bodyguard for Katniss when they go out to visit the districts, but when the group gets into the Capitol Boggs is killed by land mine when the Holo he is wearing, which detects traps fails to spot it.

Cressida

Cressida is the filmmaker in charge of taping the propaganda spots. At first Cressida thinks that it will be a good idea to have Katniss all done up for the cameras though she soon realizes that Katniss cannot give a genuine performance if she does not feel like herself. Cressida joins the rebels in their journey to the Capitol and is the one responsible for finding safety in Tigris' shop. Cressida manages to survive through the rebellion becomes someone that Katniss appreciates.

Pollux

Pollux and his brother, Castor, are two members of Cressida's camera crew though Katniss forms a closer relationship with Pollux. Pollux is an Avox and it is probable that Katniss likes him so much because he cannot speak, and also because he reminds her of Darius and Lavinia, two other Avox that Katniss knew and were killed. Pollux used to work in the Capitol so he serves as a guide through the underground. When Castor is killed Pollux is devastated, though he manages to survive.

Annie Cresta

Annie Cresta is a Hunger Games victor from District 4 who was chosen for the Quarter Quell but was replaced by Mags. We find out in Mockingjay that Mags replaced Annie because Annie and Finnick are a couple and she did not want them to go against one another. Annie was captured by the Capitol and rescued by District 13 along with Peeta and Johanna. Annie does not seem to be all-there mentally, but Finnick has a way of calming her down and bringing her into reality. Annie and Finnick are married and at the end of the novel we learn that Annie had been pregnant with Finnick's baby when he died.

Themes

Rebellion

Katniss has become the Mockingjay, the face of the rebellion of Panem. After the Quarter Quell, nearly every district of Panem is rising against the Capitol, and there are many casualties of both people and entire districts. Katniss does not have a desire to participate further in the rebellion until she sees that Peeta is being tortured by the Capitol and she launches herself into bringing them down and getting Peeta back. The rebellion, for Katniss, turns out to be not just against the Capitol but against President Coin as well after Prim is killed.

Sacrifice

Many members of the rebels were willing to put themselves in danger and sacrifice their lives for the cause, including Finnick and Prim. Sacrifice within this novel is sacrifice for a specific cause, to create a better life for those who are left behind, free from the control of a totalitarian government. There are so many players in the rebellion who act as spies and risk their own lives for the chance of bringing down President Snow and without the sacrifice of each of them individually and as a group the uprising would never have been successful.

Love

Love is an ongoing theme throughout the series but in this final installment Katniss finally understands love for the first time and knows who it is that she truly loves. As Katniss tries to remind Peeta, who he is after, he returns from the Capitol she has one moment when she is telling him about his little quirks and she has to stop because she is about to cry; this seems to be when Katniss realizes that she really does love Peeta. She refuses to allow Peeta to sacrifice himself, she refuses to leave him behind, and she is happy when he becomes the one person who follows her back to District 12.

Loss

Katniss loses a lot of people she cares about during this finale novel. She finds that Madge has died in the destruction of District 12, she loses Peeta to the Capitol at first, she loses Prim to a bomb that she thinks Gale may have created, and thus she loses Gale as well because she can no longer look at him in the same way. Katniss also loses Finnick who had become a great friend and source of comfort to her, and who also had just been married which makes his death a huge loss to Annie, as well.Finally, upon the death of Prim Mrs. Everdeen cannot bring herself to return to District 12 so Katniss loses her in a sense, as well.

Numbness

Most of the deaths in Mockingjay happen off the pages – Cinna, Madge, Peeta's family, Effie, Portia, and Peeta's prep team, to name a few. Many of the deaths that do happen within the scope of the story, like Prim's and Finnick's, seem anticlimactic and emotionless, as if they do not even matter, but that may be on purpose; in Katniss' eyes, the deaths did come out of nowhere and she has become so numb to loss at this point in her life that the audience is meant to feel her numbness, as well. There is an overall lack of emotion, as though Katniss has nothing left to give.

Success

While the rebels are absolutely successful in their mission – the presidents from both the Capitol and District 13 are taken down – it is a bittersweet success. Katniss has survived and she has managed to save both Peeta and Gale in the process, but her life will never be the same again and she has lost both Prim, the only person she is sure she ever loved, and her best friend because she feels Gale may be responsible for Prim's death. Many lives were lost in the struggle for independence so by the time it is all said and done Katniss is relieved but feels empty.

Power

While the rebel forces aim to take the power away from President Snow and to take down the Capitol they are under the power of another president, President Coin. Katniss distrusts President Coin from the very beginning and seems to understand that there is something off about the woman who controls the rebellion. Katniss, Gale, Peeta, and many others wish to be free from the control of a totalitarian government, but it seems that while in District 13 they are under the same sort of government, though on a smaller scale.

Control

The rebels have risen up out of the districts to end the control of President Snow and to be able to have freedom though they are more controlled than ever before in District 13. Katniss recognizes that 13 is quite strict as give every daily schedules, they ration food very specifically depending on who it is for, and they dictate when and where people are allowed to go, especially if it involves leaving the underground community. Katniss immediately rebels against the control in District 13, just as she does with the Capitol.

Loyalty

Despite outside influences everyone who is close to Katniss remains loyal to her rather than the Capitol or even President Coin. Katniss is the person that everyone pledges their lives to protecting and following as they feel that her determination and passion for freedom will inspire others. While Katniss seems loyal to the rebels her main goal is to kill President Snow, not to lead the rebellion. Once Katniss learns that President Coin was not loyal to her, as it was a rebel bomb which killed Prim, Katniss decides killing Coin is more important than killing Snow.

Freedom

A theme throughout the series has been freedom because it is always what Katniss is struggling to achieve. Katniss looks for freedom from starvation, freedom from the Capitol, freedom from the Hunger Games, freedom from her own confusion, and freedom from her responsibilities as the Mockingjay. While Katniss vows to kill President Snow to achieve freedom for everyone in the districts, she realizes that it is also important to kill President Coin because Katniss is sure that President Coin would have simply taken Snow's place as head of the totalitarian government.

Chapter Summaries

Chapter One

Katniss has just been rescued from the arena of the Quarter Quell by a hovercraft belonging to District 13, which was thought to have been destroyed. She finds out that the people of District 13 lived and created a community underground which is led by President Alma Coin. Katniss is in extreme shock over what she has just gone through, the new information she is being presented with, and the fact that Peeta has been taken hostage by the Capitol.

Katniss does not know how to feel about President Coin and District 13 or the rebellion. Katniss learns that Gale managed to lead a group of District 12 residents into the woods to avoid the bombing, and they made their way to District 13. The people of District 13, including the refugees from other districts, follow strict schedules, are given three meals a day, and are given jobs. Katniss is informed that Coin is only helping them because much of the population of 13 was wiped out with small pox and they need new people to breed. Katniss is informed that she is the Mockingjay, the face of the revolution, but she does not know how she feels about that responsibility.

Katniss visits District 12 and finds her home in Victor's Village still standing. She retrieves some thinks she thinks that her mother and Prim will want, including Prim's cat Buttercup. She also finds a white rose in her room that she know is left there by President Snow, and she feels his message loud and clear – he will always be watching her.

Chapter Two

Katniss learns that the Capitol knows of District 13's existence and the district probably would not survive if it were not for their extreme rationing of food and supplies. Each morning every person in 13 has a schedule for the day printed on their arm, which is washed off each night.

Katniss does not follow her schedule but spends her days exploring and hiding, which she gets away with because she has a medical bracelet that says she is "mentally disoriented". Gale has become an important figure in the rebellion and tells Katniss that they are being summoned to the command center. Once they arrive they see the television screen turn on and see Peeta sitting with Caesar Flickerman. Peeta seems to be in good health as he explains that he and Katniss had no knowledge of the rebellion and makes the announcement that the rebellion must stop because Panem is not strong or populated enough to handle it. Katniss worries that Peeta will be seen as treacherous, but she knows he is just saying what President Snow wants him to.

Katniss runs from command against Coin's orders because she does not want to hear anything negative about Peeta. Gale finds Katniss in her hiding place and tells her that he has been demoted for hitting one of Coin's men as Katniss ran from the room and also tells that Peeta was just trying to protect her by saying she did not know anything about the rebellion. Katniss realizes she must be the Mockingjay to get revenge for the destruction of District 12.

Chapter Three

The night Katniss decides to be the Mockingjay she has trouble sleeping. Prim wakes her and Katniss realizes that Prim has grown so much and is now able to comfort Katniss and talk sense to her. Prim tells Katniss that, as the Mockingjay, her role in the rebellion will be very important, and thus she will be probably be given anything she asks for, like immunity for Peeta. Katniss discusses this idea with Gale at breakfast, and they think of a few more demands.

At command, Katniss says she will be the Mockingjay, but certain demands need to be met, such as immunity for Peeta and the rest of the victors, hunting time for herself and Gale, and they be allowed to keep Buttercup. Coin agrees to all but the immunity until Katniss tells her it's her fault that Peeta was captured and not only should she grant Peeta immunity, but she should announce it publically. Plutarch and Coin's other advisors point out that Katniss has a passion that they need in their Mockingjay, and they should meet whatever demands she has because they need her, so Coin agrees.

Katniss' final demand is that when Snow is captured she can kill him herself, but Coin tells her they will have to flip a coin on that one. Plutarch and Fulvia bring Katniss and Gale to see the designs for her Mockingjay uniform, designed by Cinna before he died, tell her she will participate in propos (propaganda videos for the rebels), and bring her to a very deep level in the community where Katniss hears whimpering behind door 3908; when she gets into the room she sees her prep team.

Chapter Four

Katniss finds her prep team have been horribly beaten over stealing a piece of bread, but Katniss thinks that there is more to it, that Coin is somehow sending her a message that she is in control. Katniss and Gale are now allowed to hunt, much to Katniss' relief. Gale asks Katniss why she cares about her prep team because they are from the Capitol, and their job is to make her look nice when she heads into the bloodbath of the Hunger Games.

Katniss tells Gale they care about her and they have minds like children, though Gale does not understand because he hates everyone from the Capitol. District 13 gathers that night to hear President Coin's announcement, which will be of immunity for Peeta and other captured victors. Finnick is there, but he is still barely functioning out of sadness for his love, Annie, being held in the Capitol.

Coin explains to District 13 that Katniss did not want to join the rebellion until her demands were met, which makes some people dislike her, and immunity will only be granted as long as Katniss keeps up with her end of the deal. Katniss realizes the lives of Peeta and the others depend on her.

Chapter Five

Katniss realizes that Coin is a lot like President Snow and is just using Katniss to get what she wants. Gale thinks that this is not true, and Coin just needs to make sure the public knows that she is not allowing Katniss to manipulate her.

As the Mockingjay Katniss must be made over by her prep team who have been instructed to take her down to "beauty base zero", which means she should be naturally and flawlessly beautiful. She is dressed in the suit Cinna designed for her, but the horrific scar on her arm from where Johanna dug the tracking device out of her arm cannot be hidden, which is unfortunate because it makes people nauseous. After she is made up, she visits Beetee in the armory where he presents her with her new bow and arrows which are voice activated and can shoot fire or explosives.

Katniss thinks the new arrows may not be fair to deer, but Gale tells her that they will not be using them to shoot deer, and Katniss sees him as cold-blooded. Katniss thinks she looks very impressive in uniform, and Finnick tells her that people will either want to kill her, kiss her, or be her. When it comes time for Katniss to deliver her line, Haymitch cracks up laughing because Katniss is less than convincing. He tells her that her performance would end a revolution.

Chapter Six

Haymitch calls a meeting in the command center and tells everyone that Katniss' performance is not going to work. He says that Katniss must be thrown into an actual combat situation so her words and actions can be real. Coin agrees, though not whole-heartedly, and decides they must tell the public that Katniss lost the baby she is supposed to be carrying in her escape from the Games.

Katniss speaks to Haymitch alone and tells him she is upset that he did not save Peeta; Haymitch tells her he cannot believe she ever left Peeta's side. Katniss learns her first mission will be in District 8 and in preparation for the mission Katniss is dressed in her suit and make-up free, to Fulvia's disappointment. Finnick wants to come, but Katniss knows he is not ready so she sends him to see Beetee for his new trident.Katniss meets with Plutarch who tells her that most of the districts are in revolt except District 2 from which many people have volunteered as peacekeepers.

Plutarch tells Katniss the purpose of the rebellion is to form a democracy which, Haymitch jokes, has only worked in books. Finally, Katniss is given a pill called "nightlock" which will kill her instantly and is only to be taken if she is captured.

Chapter Seven

Katniss arrives in District 8 accompanied by Boggs, Gale, Cressida, the cameramen, and the bodyguards; and Haymitch will be giving instructions from the hovercraft via earpiece. They find that many people are injured due to Capitol bombs and have all been herded into a single location, which Gale finds unsettling. The group meets Paylor, who is the head of the District 8 rebellion.

Katniss is brought in to see the wounded and spends time talking to them, though most just want to ask how she and Peeta are or just hold her hand for a second. Haymitch tells Katniss that the bombers are coming back, and they do not have time to get her out so the group will have to hide; he does not think the bombers know the Mockingjay is there.

The bombers go straight for the wounded and Katniss realizes that Gale had already figured out the plan, as soon as he had seen that the wounded had all been grouped together. Despite the urging that they stay hidden Katniss rips out her earpiece and she and Gale begin shooting at the Capitol hovercrafts; they take down a couple bombers but cannot save the hospital which is housing the wounded. Katniss is furious as she knows President Snow has sent a message so she looks into the camera and sends him one back, "the fire is catching".

Chapter Eight

After Katniss' adrenaline rush is over she begins to feel her injuries and throws up on Boggs' vest as he carries her to the hovercraft. Katniss awakens in the hospital of District 13 to her mother caring for her. Mrs. Everdeen is very upset that no one told her Katniss was going into a combat zone, and Katniss feels guilty.

The propaganda team has managed to hack into the Capitol's broadcasting to air their first propo and thinks that they need to film more battle scenes, though more calculated ones. Fulvia has an idea to do propos called "we remember" that showcase those who have died in the Games. Katniss returns to the hospital and is visited by Haymitch who tells her that he will have an earpiece surgically implanted if she tries to ignore him again.

A Capitol propo flickers on the television and Katniss sees Peeta being interviewed by Caesar Flickerman again, though Peeta now looks awful. Peeta urges Katniss not to trust the people in District 13, but Finnick tells her to pretend she never saw it, which is exactly what she does when Fulvia and Plutarch come in to check on her.

Chapter Nine

Katniss and Finnick pretend they did not see Peeta's message, but Katniss does wonder if she can trust the people in 13, as none of them including Gale, told her about the propo. When Katniss confronts Gale he tells her he did not mention it because he was worried about Katniss' health. For the next rebel, propo Katniss and Gale will be taken back to District 12, though Katniss has a hard time performing for the cameras because she is so hurt by the wreckage she sees.

Katniss wants to go into the woods, and the camera crew follows her. Cressida decides to take a break from filming, and Katniss begins to sing to the mockingjays in the trees, at Pollux's request, a song called "The Hanging Tree"; which her father taught her, but her mother forbade her to sing because it is about a man who has been hung requesting for his lover to join him on the gallows.

As Katniss sings the mockingjays sing back, which the cameramen are sure to get footage of much to Plutarch's joy. Katniss stops at her house in Victor's Village to grab a few things and Gale reminds her of the time she kissed him while he was sick. As Gale gets emotional Katniss kisses him again, as Gale knew she would because she always responds when others are in pain. Gale feels that his pain is the only thing that grabs Katniss' attention. Back at command the rebels set in to watch a Capitol propo, and find that President Snow is on the screen with an awful looking Peeta.

Beetee tries to hack into the signal and just before he does Katniss hears the warning from Peeta that she and District 13 will be dead by the morning. The cameras around Peeta are sent to the ground, and all Katniss can see is Peeta's blood on the floor as she hears him screaming.

Chapter Ten

Haymitch and Katniss are the only people worried about Peeta; everyone else wonders if Peeta's warning is true. Haymitch tells Coin that he would not make up something like that though Coin is skeptical. Coin issues an alert, just in case, that sends all of the inhabitants of District 13 to a bunker very deep in the ground.

Once in the shelter Plutarch tells Katniss that she must remain strong for the others and though she is furious that he referred to Peeta's warning as a "setback" she maintains her calm. Katniss reads the instructions in her sleeping area and heads over to get her supplies; she realizes that she is the first one to get supplies and everyone else follows her lead.

As Katniss sets up the bunk and Mrs. Everdeen arrives she realizes that Prim is not there, nor is Buttercup so Katniss thinks Prim must have gone back for the cat. At the last moment, Prim, Gale, and Buttercup arrive and then the bombing begins. In the bunker, they can feel shaking from the bombs but are perfectly safe. Katniss ask Prim how she likes life in 13 and Prim admits that they are training her to be a doctor.

Katniss tells Prim that she is worried about Peeta, though Prim believes that they will not kill Peeta or they will have nothing to use against Katniss.

Chapter Eleven

As Katniss is playing a game with Buttercup, in which he chases a flashlight beam along the floor and wall, she realizes how President Snow is using her and Peeta. Katniss is the cat and Peeta is the beam of light; she will chase him all over, and when she cannot catch him she will sit and wait until she can because she cannot leave him alone. Katniss goes to see Finnick and tells him that she has finally figured it out; Finnick is sorry he did not explain it to her earlier but tells her that Snow is doing the same thing with Annie.

Katniss and Finnick sit there together aimlessly knotting pieces of rope and Gale eyes them with jealousy. After the bombing, Katniss heads to the surface to film another propo; she finds two dozen roses and knows they are a message from Snow. Katniss does not know what to say so Cressida tries doing a Q&A session with her; Katniss is only able to answer one question before her voice breaks. Katniss does not know if she can be the Mockingjay if Peeta keeps being tortured.

Later Haymitch tells Katniss that a rescue mission has been planned to get Peeta out of the Capitol; the only reason it was not attempted before is because of the risk factor. Katniss learns that Gale was the first to volunteer for the mission and fearfully realizes she could lose Gale and Peeta both at the same time.

Chapter Twelve

Katniss wants to join the mission to rescue Peeta, but Haymitch tells her they have already left. Haymitch says that if Katniss can bring herself to film another propo then they can probably break into the Capitol's broadcast system and use the propo as a means of distracting President Snow during the rescue. Katniss and Finnick both decide to film propos; Katniss starts talking to the camera about the first time she ever met Peeta, the night he gave her the burned bread.

Katniss realized that Peeta had loved her even then. Katniss explains that all the districts have to do to defeat the Capitol is to declare their independence because the Capitol cannot survive without support from the districts. When it is Finnick's turn he tells the camera about how President Snow sold him as a prostitute after he won the games and many of the rich people he slept with told him secrets. Many of the secrets detail Snow's rise to power, and the fact that he poisoned his opponents so he would always win; Snow even ingested some of the poison himself, which is why his mouth is always bleeding, from open blisters.

Katniss as Haymitch if he was sold to people as well, but Haymitch says President Snow made an example of him by killing off his family and his girlfriend. When the rescue mission comes back Gale is injured, Annie is reunited with Finnick, Johanna is with them, and when Katniss runs into to see Peeta he strangles her.

Chapter Thirteen

Katniss is back in the hospital while her throat heals and both she and Haymitch are shocked by Peeta's actions. Plutarch and Beetee believe that in the Capitol Peeta's mind was "hijacked" with the venom of trackerjackers, which means he was conditioned and brainwashed into believing that Katniss is the enemy.

They are going to try their best to bring Peeta back to normal, but they warn Katniss that they can make no promises and he will have a hard time knowing what of his memories are real, and what has been implanted by the Capitol. Katniss breaks down and has to be sedated. Once Katniss is released from the hospital she is again wearing a "mentally disoriented" bracelet.

Katniss learns that Gale and Beetee have been forming a series of snares that will be used to play on human emotions, which Katniss thinks is unfair. The doctors decide to bring Delly Cartwright from District 12 in to see Peeta because they want to awaken some of his memories without triggering any of Katniss. Peeta starts to ask Delly questions about District 12 and goes off about how it is Katniss' fault everyone is dead, and she is a mutt created by the government to destroy him. Delly tries to stand up for Katniss but is taken from the room.

Katniss asks to be sent somewhere else because she cannot stand being around Peeta; she is sent to District 2 where the rebels are starting to take over but are having a hard time.

Chapter Fourteen

It has been two weeks since Katniss has been sent to District 2 and she finds herself filming propos whenever she can to keep her mind off Peeta. She has not been involved with any fighting but is allowed in on strategy meetings. In District two, there is a fortress buried inside the mountains where the Capitol people stay; it is referred to as "The Nut". The Nut is comprised of many tunnels and train tracks that has proven, thus far, to be impenetrable making it difficult for the rebels to get a stronghold.

Beetee and Gale begin to develop a strategy to break into The Nut and decide that they must block the entrances and trap everyone inside, killing them; Katniss does not like the plan because it means they have to be willing to kill everyone who is inside The Nut.

In District 13, the doctors are working on Peeta and Plutarch tells Katniss that he is improving, though Haymitch admits that his improvements are not significant. Prim has the idea to subject Peeta to the venom of the trackerjackers again but to expose him to positive memories of Katniss while he is hallucinating; a sort of reverse "hijacking" that thus far has only left Peeta confused.

Chapter Fifteen

Gale argues in favor of his strategy to bring down The Nut despite the mixed feelings people are having about it, making the point that the Capitol was not trying to spare the lives of anyone in District 12 when they destroyed it. The council decides to use Gale's plan but to leave the train track opening at the bottom of the mountain open so give some of the people a chance to surrender.

The District 13 hovercraft launches its bombs, which causes the avalanche that will trap everyone inside. As Katniss watches The Nut crumble, she is horrified and remembers the day her father died in the mine explosion. Haymitch tries to comfort Katniss through her earpiece by telling her that Peeta is making progress; they showed Peeta the video of Katniss singing to the mockingjays and he remembered hearing Katniss' father sing it in his parents' bakery.

The connection to Katniss should have caused a meltdown in Peeta but did not. Cressida tells Katniss that she is expected to make a speech urging people to join with the rebels, but just as she is about to she sees the survivors coming out of The Nut, and they are armed. Katniss pleads with them to join forces in the rebellion; just as Katniss thinks her speech may be working she sees herself being shot on live television.

Chapter Sixteen

Katniss wakes up in the hospital of District 13 and sees Johanna Mason next to her. Johanna takes Katniss' morphling drip and puts it in her own arm, explaining to Katniss that she does it often, and life would be much easier if she could just live in a morphling haze all the time. Katniss does not complain because Johanna saved her in the Games only to be captured and tortured by the Capitol.

Johanna tells Katniss that she was shot, but the bullet did not penetrate her skin because her mockingjay suit stopped it; she ended up with just badly bruised ribs. Johanna leaves the room when Gale comes and he and Katniss discuss their difference of opinion in District 2; Katniss thinks Gale's plan was no better than the Capitol bombing the hospital in District 8 and Gale thinks that because the bombers came from District 2 he was preventing more bombings from happening.

Katniss meets with Plutarch, and he tells her that the Capitol is officially cut off from the districts now that 2 has been taken down; they are going to film some entertainment propos to rub their livelihood in the face of President Snow. The entertainment will take place in the form of a wedding – for Finnick and Annie, not Peeta and Katniss. Katniss sees the wedding cake and recognizes the frosting as Peeta's work; she realizes that he is making more progress than she thought. He asks to see her, and she goes to him though she is not prepared for all the mean things he says to her; he says she is not very pretty or nice ,and criticizes her for kisses both him and Gale. Katniss leaves the room and hides, very upset that Peeta has finally seen her the way she sees herself.

Chapter Seventeen

Katniss finds out that the rebels are set to attack the Capitol, and she has not been invited though Gale has. Coin explains to her that Gale has attended all of his training sessions and Katniss has not ever attended one but perhaps Katniss will be flown in after the hard part is done.

Katniss makes a deal with Coin that her participation will be considered again before the trip if she attends all of her training sessions from then on. Johanna is angry that she was not invited either so the two girls decide they are going to work together to push through training in the hopes that they will be allowed to go, though both girls are in rough shape at first. Katniss gets a painful injection that works to speed up her healing process and Johanna deals with morphling withdrawals. Katniss and Johanna move out of the hospital so they are not seen as patients and become roommates in a room across the hall from Mrs. Everdeen and Prim. Johanna never showers but only washes off with a damp cloth, which Katniss does not understand.

One night while Katniss is eating dinner with her group of friends Peeta asks to join them; Katniss is alarmed at how easily Peeta's mood can change from kind to vindictive. Katniss tells Gale she thinks that Peeta sees her as she really is but Gale thinks she is crazy.

Chapter Eighteen

It is time for Katniss and Johanna to take their training exams to see if they are fit for combat. Katniss sails through the first three sections but is worried for the fourth section where she will be tested on her weaknesses. She finds herself in a situation where the commander tells her to get down when she thinks that she could solve the problem single-handedly, but she knows that is her weakness so she listens and drops to the ground; Katniss passes her test. Katniss becomes a member of Bogg's team, Squad 451, along with Gale and Finnick.

The team is supposed to be sharpshooters, but Plutarch tells them they are the "star squad" which means they are to stay out of harm's way and be the publicity team. Katniss immediately starts to form a plan that involves getting away from her squad and to President Snow. Johanna did not make a team because she failed her weakness test which involved water; Katniss learns that Johanna was tortured with electrical currents through water in the Capitol and that is why she never showers. To comfort Johanna Katniss wraps some pine needles in a bandage and brings it to Johanna to remind her of what her home smelled like. Johanna is comforted and makes Katniss swear she will kill Snow.

The job of Squad 451 is to take out pods in the Capitol that are traps to kill intruders. When Peeta joins the team he tells them that Coin has sent him to add heat to the propos, but Katniss thinks that he was sent to kill her.

Chapter Nineteen

Katniss tells Boggs that she thinks Peeta has been sent to kill her but Boggs disagrees, though he tells her he will do what he can to protect her just in case. Boggs explains to Katniss that she is a threat to Coin because she does not know if she would support Coin's rise to power after Snow is taken down so Katniss may be best served as a martyr for the rebellion.

People are having a hard time trusting Peeta, and he feels uncomfortable though Katniss treats him worse than anyone else; Haymitch tells Katniss that if the tables were turned Peeta would never treat her the way she has been treating him. One night Peeta admits that he has a hard time knowing what is real in his head and what is not so the squad agrees to help him figure it out and lets him ask questions whenever he needs to.

Peeta shares painful memories from the Capitol sometimes, such as watching an Avox be tortured, and explains that the memories that are real are usually the ones that are not "shiny". Katniss tries to help Peeta remember by telling him that his favorite color is orange, though not bright orange but the orange of a sunset. She also tells him "You're a painter. You're a baker. You like to sleep with the windows open. You never take sugar in your tea. And you always double-knot your shoe laces." Then Katniss runs into her tent before she cries. When they continue on, Boggs checks his Holo, a device that shows where the pods are though it does not show all of them. One of the unseen pods takes out a sharpshooter and the other takes off Boggs' legs.

Chapter Twenty

As Boggs is dying he programs his Holo to give primary clearance to Katniss, though she does not understand why. Before Boggs dies he whispers to Katniss to not trust anyone, do what she came to do, and kill Peeta. As they escape the rapidly exploding pods a wave of black goo comes over the street and Peeta goes mad again, trying to smash Katniss in the head. As one of the squad tries to hold Peeta back Peeta kicks him, and he goes flying into another pod which burns him to death.

The group decides to leave Boggs because they know he cannot survive and Jackson, the second-in-command, demands the Holo, but Katniss tells her that it has been transferred to her command and she is in charge now.Katniss tells Jackson that Coin has sent her to kill Snow; though everyone knows that it not the truth they go along with it. The group trudges through the black goo and takes refuge in another nearby home when an emergency broadcast comes onto the television; the broadcast shows Katniss' squad dodging pods and announces that they are all dead.

Katniss feels that the announcement is beneficial to the squad, but she knows that the people back in District 13 will not know the truth and be devastated. Peeta has been knocked unconscious since he attacked Katniss and he starts to come to only to suggest to everyone that they should kill him.

Chapter Twenty-One

Peeta tries to convince the squad that he will be a hindrance to them, and they should give him a suicide pill, but they tell him that he is going to stay alive and stay with them. Another emergency broadcast comes on, and President Snow announces that Katniss' death means a change in the war and an impossibility of victory for the rebels. Snow is interrupted by a broadcast from District 13 in which President Coin urges the rebels to remember their Mockingjay and to fight in her memory.

The squad looks at the Holo to choose a route and finds that the underground tunnels have less pods than there are aboveground. Pollux was forced to work in the sewers for a few years so he knows his way around the underground and serves as their leader. Once down in the tunnels they stop to rest and Katniss talks to Peeta about his "shiny" memories because she remembers what the hallucinations from trackerjacker venom are like and thinks she knows what he means.

Peeta explains that the fake memories have a shiny quality to them while the real memories do not. Katniss admits to Peeta that she is still trying to protect him, as always. As Katniss and Pollux are waking everyone up to continue on, Katniss hears a sound hissing her name.

Chapter Twenty-Two

Katniss hears Peeta begin to hiss her name as well and realizes that he is reverting back to his Capitol thinking. Just as Katniss is about to kill Peeta with her bow and arrow he snaps back into reality and tells her to run. Capitol Mutts are running after the squad, and Katniss makes sure everyone is armed as they take off. Katniss can smell the scent of roses which sickens her as she associates it with President Snow.

The squad runs into some peacekeepers and manages to kill the first wave of them; the second wave of peacekeepers is taken down by the Mutts, hybrid lizard-humans with long tails. Peeta takes charge and holds everyone together through the Mutt attack, but he suddenly starts to lose control until Katniss calms him down. Katniss asks Peeta if he will be there for her, and he says "always", just as the old Peeta would say. Katniss decides they must get to the surface and urges everyone to run with her though she realizes that one by one she is losing members of her squad who are staying behind to make sure Katniss survives.

As Katniss is about to break the surface she looks down and sees that Finnick is fighting off three mutts himself – and then he falls. Katniss cannot leave Finnick to suffer at the hands of the Mutts so she takes off her Holo, whispers "nightlock, nightlock, nightlock", and throws it down to where she last saw Finnick, knowing that it will explode and take him out of his misery. As Katniss, Peeta, Gale, Pollux, and Cressida break the surface a woman spots them, but Katniss kills her before she can say anything.

Chapter Twenty-Three

Katniss feels bad for killing the woman, but she has no time to think about it because the crowd walking around outside is searching for Katniss and the others. The group searches the closets in the dead woman's house and disguise themselves with clothing and makeup to look like they belong in the Capitol.

Cressida, being from the Capitol, knows exactly where they are and helps them navigate through the streets. Cressida leads the group to a fur undergarments shop in which Katniss sees Tigris, a woman who used to be a stylist in the Games and has had her face surgically altered to represent a tiger. Cressida tells Tigris that Plutarch sent them to her, and she leads them to a secret entrance to her basement, which the naked eye would never know existed. Katniss worries that their mission is failing, but Gale assures her everything is going fine, and they remember their plan to assassinate Snow.

While Katniss is trying to sleep that night she hears Gale and Peeta talking about her, and who they think she really loves. Peeta assumes she loves Gale because she has known him for so long and Gale says she definitely loves Peeta because she has never kissed him the way she kisses Peeta. Peeta asks who Gale thinks Katniss will choose, and Gale says that knowing Katniss she will choose whoever she knows she cannot survive without.

Chapter Twenty-Four

Katniss is insulted by Gale's comment as she thinks that she would have no problem surviving without either of them. As many refugees are coming into the Capitol, those who live there or have shops are being asked to share them. The group knows they must leave the shop, well-disguised, because it is only a matter of time before Tigris is asked to take in refugees.

Tigris dresses the five of them in the best disguises she can and they head out; Pollux and Cressida first, the Katniss and Gale, and finally Peeta trailing to create a diversion if he needs to. Gale gives Peeta his nightlock pill just in case he is captured, insisting that if he is captured Katniss will be able to shoot him. As Katniss and Gale head toward the mansion, they have to steer clear of peacekeepers and avoid pods.

One pod causes the sidewalk to open underneath them, and Katniss barely pulls herself up onto the flat ground. She sees that Gale is still hanging, and she shoots open the door above him so he can swing up but there are peacekeepers inside and they capture Gale. Gale mouths to Katniss to shoot him but she does not understand him until it is too late and he is pulled inside. Katniss knows her only chance of saving Gale is to get to the mansion.

Once she arrives she sees that President Snow has gathered a large group of children at the front of his mansion, which she assumes is to offer protection to him. Parachutes are dropped down to the kids with what they assume are gifts, but they contain explosives. The rebels medics along go in to help the children and Katniss sees the long braid of Prim's hair in the group right before the parachutes explode again but bigger this time, killing Prim.

Chapter Twenty-Five

As Katniss runs forward to try to save Prim, she catches fire. As Katniss burns, she thinks of Prim and drifts off to unconsciousness. Katniss wakes in a hospital hears the doctors saying that while she is not physically unable to speak she seems unwilling, as though she has become a "mental Avox".

Katniss is filled in on what has happened; the war ended with the parachute bombs, Coin is now president, Peeta is also recovering from burns, and Gale has already gone back into the field after being shot twice by peacekeepers. Snow was put to trial, found guilty, and sentenced to execution though they are waiting for Katniss to carry it out. As Katniss is wandering around the mansion one day, where the rebels have now set up house, she smells President Snow's roses. She sees guards posted outside of a room and asks if she can go inside despite the fact that Coin forbade it. Paylor, the leader from District 8, allows her in, and Katniss looks for a rose to pin in Snow's lapel before she kills him.

As she picks out a rose, Katniss is startled by Snow's voice, as he is in the room with her. Snow tells Katniss he is sorry about Prim and fills her in on the information that Coin ordered the bombing, not him. Katniss does not want to believe Snow, but she cannot help to remember the traps that Gale and Beetee had been forming that would prey on human emotions. Snow tells Katniss that it was Coin's plan all along to take over control of Panem, and she used Snow and Katniss as her pawns. Katniss accuses him of lying, but he reminds her that long ago the two of them vowed never to lie to one another.

Chapter Twenty-Six

Katniss is confused and troubled by what Snow has told her and does not know whether to believe him. She tries to speak to Haymitch, but he is very drunk. When Katniss asks Gale whether it was his trap that killed Prim he admits that he does not know. Gale knows that the possibility that his trap killed Prim has taken away any chance that he and Katniss can ever be together because she will never look at him the same again.

Katniss has to get ready for Snow's execution and her prep team is instructed to bring her to "beauty base zero" again though it is difficult because she is so badly burned and scarred. Katniss' prep team is the only one that survived the war. Coin gathers the remaining Hunger Games victors together, there are only seven of them, and asks whether they should host one last Hunger Games with the children of the Capitol as tributes.

The vote is 4-3 in favor of the Games, with Johanna, Enobaria, Katniss, and Haymitch all voting in favor, "for Prim". Coin is very pleased. Katniss is brought in to kill President Snow with her one, single arrow, and, as she faces him, she remembers their agreement not to lie to one another. Katniss takes aim and with her one last arrow shoots President Coin dead.

Chapter Twenty-Seven

Katniss tries to get to her nightlock pill knowing she will be killed for her assassination of President Coin but finds that Peeta's hand is keeping her from getting into the pocket. Katniss sees and hears Snow laughing as blood streams from his mouth, and he chokes on it; she knows he will die too. Katniss is subdued and days later is informed by Plutarch as to what has happened; her trial has already come and gone and she was pardoned due to her mental state.

Katniss and Haymitch are sent back to District 12 and Haymitch asks Katniss if she wants to know who is not going back but she says she would rather be surprised. Greasy Sae comes back and checks in on Katniss sometimes as she is alone in her house; Mrs. Everdeen decided not to return but to immerse herself in her work because Prim's memory is too painful. Slowly people come back to District 12, but Gale does not, instead he gets a job in District 2 and Katniss assumes that he will fall in love with someone else now. Peeta does return, and he helps Katniss to deal with her grief and recover.

Buttercup returns to the house, having come all the way from District 13, and he and Katniss mourn Prim together as Buttercup seems to understand that Prim is gone. Over time, Katniss and Peeta create a memory book together, she remembers people and things and Peeta paints pictures of her memories, including a photo of Finnick's son which Annie has just given birth to.

Katniss slowly realizes that she and Gale were too much alike to have worked together, they are both fiery. Katniss knows that what she needed was not Gale's fire but Peeta's warmth and goodness. Katniss finally admits to Peeta that she loves him. In the epilogue, Katniss reveals that she and Peeta have gotten married and had two children of their own, though their children will never have to worry about the Hunger Games because they no longer exist.

About BookCaps

We all need refreshers every now and then. Whether you are a student trying to cram for that big final, or someone just trying to understand a book more, BookCaps can help. We are a small, but growing company, and are adding titles every month.

Visit www.bookcaps.com to see more of our books, or contact us with any questions.

Made in the USA
San Bernardino, CA
11 April 2013